MAN'S INHUMANITIES

TORTURE

By Charles E. Pederson

ERICKSON PRESS
Yankton, South Dakota

For more information, contact:
Erickson Press
329 Broadway
PO Box 33
Yankton, SD 57078
Or you can visit our Web site at **www.ericksonpress.com**

Content Consultant:
Professor Mark Bernstein
Joyce and Edward E. Brewer Chair in Applied Ethics
Philosophy Department, Purdue University

Editor: Amy Van Zee
Copy Editor: Paula Lewis
Design and Production: Becky Daum

Library of Congress Cataloging-in-Publication Data
Pederson, Charles E.
  Torture / by Charles E. Pederson.
      p. cm. — (Man's inhumanities)
  Includes bibliographical references (p.) and index.
  ISBN 978-1-60217-974-5 (alk. paper)
1. Torture. I. Title. II. Series.

  HV8593.P43 2009
  364.6′7—dc22

                                          2008034830

CONTENTS

A TORTURE SCENE

*T*he prisoner's hands and feet were tied tightly. Chains hung from his wrists, and a cloth bag covered his head. He could smell the damp concrete floor. The cold cinder blocks pressed painfully into his back. He could hear the guards laughing down the corridor. A steel door banged shut somewhere.

His cell was at the end of the hall. It was past the other prisoners. The sound of footsteps approached without stopping. He knew someone was coming for him. The prisoner flinched as the guards flung open his cell door. They shouted something at him, but he did not understand. He did not speak their language. But he did not need a translator to understand the anger in their voices. Two guards hauled him to his feet. Each guard tightly gripped an arm. They removed the prisoner's clothing.

They pushed the prisoner down the hall, kicking him when he stumbled. He knew some of his fellow prisoners had been beaten on the soles of their feet. Others had been forced to kneel for hours while extremely loud music was played. It kept the prisoners from making sense of what went on around them.

The man was terrified. He did not know what was going to happen to him. He imagined being beaten, whipped, burned, or cut. He imagined all kinds of physical agonies caused by torture. The fear alone was torture.

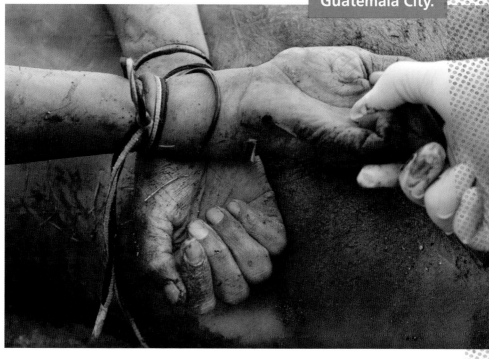

An adolescent male found tortured and disfigured in Guatemala City.

A Current Issue

This incident did not happen to a real person. However, people have been put in similar situations.

There are many types of torture. One can imagine a dungeon filled with iron equipment. These instruments caused a great deal of pain until the victims confessed to their crimes. Often the torture happened whether or not they were guilty.

Most people do not think torture still happens. Some choose not to think about it at all, because it is an unpleasant topic. But torture occurs all over the world. It is hard to know how many men, women, and children are tortured every year. The issue is not always exposed to the public. Most certainly, there are thousands of people who are tortured.

But recently, torture has been in the news. It is discussed in regard to military operations in Iraq, Afghanistan, and other places. Movies and TV dramas may show torture scenes. People talk about it, trying to decide whether it is good or bad depending on the situation. One thing is clear—torture is a big issue.

Chapter 1

WHAT IS TORTURE?

What exactly defines torture? Part of torture is to cause someone physical pain. But is that enough? Consider a person riding a bike who runs into someone by accident. The victim is hurt. No one would argue that the victim was tortured.

According to the *World Book Encyclopedia*, causing pain is only part of torture's definition. The encyclopedia adds that torture is the "intentional infliction of mental or physical pain."[1] But even that definition may not be enough. There are situations where someone causes pain, but the person receiving it is willing. For example, a century ago, dentists had no anesthesia. They had to work on people's teeth without any medicine to reduce the pain. Yet, the patient willingly underwent the pain of dental work to avoid rotten teeth. Many medical procedures caused awful pain for patients. Yet, no one argued that this was true torture.

The UN Convention against Torture and Other Cruel, Inhuman or Degrading Treatment or Punishment (UNCAT) defines torture. This convention agrees that torture is the infliction of mental and physical pain. It also adds that there are purposes behind torture. These may include punishment. Or, torture may be an attempt to get information. Finally, to qualify as torture, a torturer must have the permission "of a public official or other person acting in an official capacity."[2]

Sound Torture

According to the BBC, captives in Iraq were subjected to sound torture. They were deprived of sleep. They were also forced to listen to loud music for long periods of time. The songs included the themes from the children's shows *Sesame Street* and *Barney*. Their captors thought that doing these things would make the prisoners more likely to talk. Many people said that this treatment could be considered torture.

Many imagine torture happening in a dark basement or dungeon.

The *Stanford Encyclopedia of Philosophy* provides a more complete definition. It gives three conditions that must be met for an action to be called torture.

First, torture is the "intentional infliction of extreme physical suffering" on a defenseless person.[3] The person being tortured is not willing to take the pain. He or she is also unable to avoid the pain. For example, the person may be strapped to a chair and unable to move.

Second, torture intends to limit a victim's independence as a human. That is, the person cannot decide to get away from the torture. Force is usually involved. At the very root of torture is the idea of robbing someone's independence.

Third, torture is performed "for the purpose of breaking the victim's will."[5] No matter what the victim wants to do, the extreme pain is intended to cause the individual to do whatever the torturer wants.

There is a recent addition to the definition. It notes that torture may be used to create fear in an entire community. This use of torture causes people not to act against the torturers for fear it could happen to them, too. Germany under Nazi rule provides a good

These Jewish prisoners were burned alive in a Nazi concentration camp. This Army official brought German civilians to the camp to show them what the Nazis had done.

example of this. Many people were very afraid of being noticed by the government. So, they did not protest the arrest and torture of innocent people. A more modern example occurred in Iraq under Saddam Hussein. As in Nazi Germany, many Iraqis were afraid of being arrested and tortured. As a result, they didn't speak up against the government's actions.

If you follow the UNCAT's definitions of torture, you can consider how torture is used as part of government policy and action as well as that of other institutions. Torture has been used to gain information and to change people's behavior and thinking.

People are tortured for many reasons. Amnesty International notes that people are tortured because they are "activists for human rights, labor rights, or any other cause, because they are family members

Gestapo

During the 1930s and 1940s, the Gestapo was organized in Adolf Hitler's Germany. Its name comes from the German *geheime Staatspolizei* or "secret state police." Along with controlling Germany, the Gestapo was also active in conquered countries in Europe. Its stated purpose was to control people suspected of being disloyal to Germany. It acted on its own without holding trials or giving its prisoners any rights. The Gestapo was feared for its use of torture and for the disappearance of German citizens who vanished without anyone knowing for sure what had happened to them.

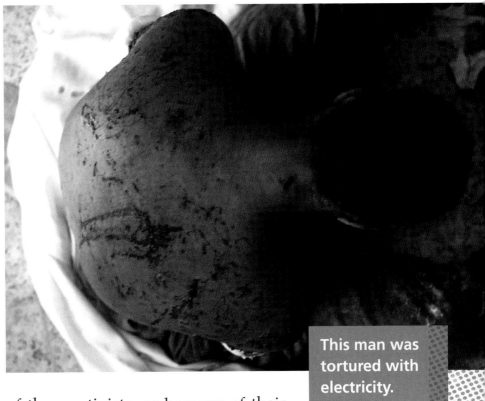

This man was tortured with electricity.

of these activists, or because of their identity (ethnicity, gender, sexual identity, etc.)."[6] Kathy Turman, Director of the U.S. Justice Department's Office for Victims of Crime, claims "tens of thousands of people fall victim to the ravages of torture every year. An estimated 400,000 torture survivors live in the United States today. Studies have estimated that up to 30 percent of all refugees are torture survivors."[7]

Turman points out that many refugees leaving their countries because of war have been tortured. She states that "torture survivors represent an 'invisible'

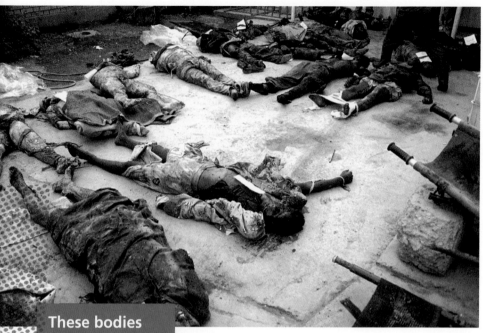

These bodies were found near Baghdad, Iraq, in 2007. They show signs of torture.

population in communities across the United States. Torture is a painful, shaming, and humiliating experience; it is extraordinarily difficult for survivors to talk about what happened to them. . . . Consequently, survivors fear that they will not be believed."[8]

This issue has been around for thousands of years. But it is clear that politically motivated torture is still in practice today.

Chapter 2

A HISTORY OF TORTURE

*A*ncient civilizations used torture. This included the Greeks, Egyptians, and Persians. Torture's use began as a form of questioning suspected criminals. In the Roman world, it was used as a method of retrieving truth from people of low status. Eventually, torture also became associated with punishment.

In about 400 CE, the Roman emperor declared Christianity the official religion of the Roman Empire. This meant that anyone who disagreed was committing a crime against the Roman emperor. Those who openly disagreed with official religious teachings were called heretics. These people were seen as acting in ways that upset the law and order of society. The Roman government punished heretics with torture.

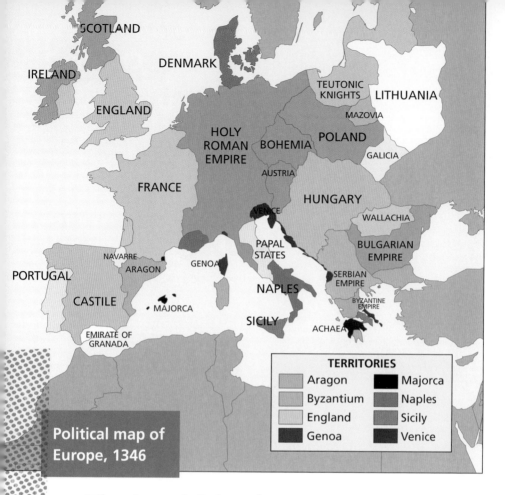

Map labels: SCOTLAND, IRELAND, DENMARK, ENGLAND, TEUTONIC KNIGHTS, LITHUANIA, MAZOVIA, HOLY ROMAN EMPIRE, BOHEMIA, POLAND, GALICIA, AUSTRIA, FRANCE, HUNGARY, VENICE, WALLACHIA, NAVARRE, PAPAL STATES, BULGARIAN EMPIRE, GENOA, SERBIAN EMPIRE, PORTUGAL, ARAGON, NAPLES, CASTILE, MAJORCA, SICILY, ACHAEA, BYZANTINE EMPIRE, EMIRATE OF GRANADA

TERRITORIES

Aragon		Majorca	
Byzantium		Naples	
England		Sicily	
Genoa		Venice	

Political map of Europe, 1346

The Inquisition in Europe

Most people think of torture in connection with Europe in the Middle Ages. This time is also known as the medieval period, from approximately 400 to 1400 CE. But European societies then were more accepting of torture than people are today. Governments and authority figures saw torture as a way to gather information or confessions.

During the European Inquisition in the Middle Ages, judges studied a person's religious beliefs. They wanted to make sure the person was Christian.

"The Hammer of Witches"

During the Middle Ages, many people feared witches and witchcraft. One book, the *Malleus Maleficarum* ("The Hammer of Witches"), described how to catch and test those who were suspected to be witches. It describes many types of torture that may be employed to cause accused witches to confess. One passage notes that if, after torture, "the prisoner will not confess the truth satisfactorily, other sorts of tortures must be placed before him, with the statement that unless he will confess the truth, he must endure these also."[1]

After a time, government officials stopped punishing offenders, and "the church took over the role."[2] By the early 1230s, the Roman Catholic Church set up special courts and judges to battle heresy. These were beliefs that went against the doctrines of the church. The judges were usually religious brothers or monks. They were allowed to question suspected heretics to force them to change their beliefs. At this time in Europe, the Roman Catholic Church was much more powerful in everyday life than it is today. Few people questioned the purposes and methods of the Inquisition.

In this torture device, called the head crusher, the victim's chin is placed on the lower bar and the cap is lowered by twisting the crank.

The Spanish Inquisition

The Spanish Inquisition began in 1478. This was separate from the Inquisition in the rest of Europe. The Spanish kings, not the pope, controlled the Spanish Inquisition. The Spanish Inquisition also had a different purpose. It originally attempted to discover secret Jews who publicly claimed to be Christians. By the 1500s, its power had increased so much that people considered saints today were investigated for heresy. This included Saint Ignatius and Saint Teresa of Ávila.

The inquisitors (investigators) of the Spanish Inquisition were well known for their brutal tortures.

Torquemada

Tomas de Torquemada led the Spanish Inquisition. He was born in 1420 in Valladolid, Spain. Torquemada became a Dominican friar. He became the head of the Spanish Inquisition in 1483. He was very influential with Queen Isabella and King Ferdinand. They gave Christopher Columbus money to try to find a new route to India. Torquemada created a royal order in 1492. This law forced several hundred thousand Jews out of Spain. Under Torquemada, "the Spanish Inquisition was much harsher, more highly organized, and far freer with the death penalty than the medieval Inquisition."[3]

In particular, the Spanish Inquisition held hundreds of *autos-da-fé* (Portuguese for "acts of faith"). An auto-da-fé included the burning alive of confessed heretics. It has been estimated that the Spanish Inquisition tortured and executed nearly 2,000 people from the 1480s until about 1500. The Spanish Inquisition lasted until 1834.

Methods and Techniques in the Middle Ages

Whipping and beating are common methods of torture. But some methods include fire or iron implements that slowly tear and break bodies. People have also been tortured by the rack. This device stretches people's arms and legs until their bones

Auto-Da-Fé

The *auto-da-fé* was a day intended specifically for the examination of "heretics." Those not freed were burned. Inquisitors burned their victims because they were forbidden to "shed blood." A Roman Catholic concept is *"Ecclesia non novit sanguinem"* (the church does not know blood).

The rack became a standard method of torture beginning in ancient Egypt.

become dislocated at the joints. One torture victim described the skin being peeled from his feet. He was hung by his arms from hooks in the ceiling. "Sometimes they put me onto a torture table and stretched me out . . . which gave me the feeling that they were going to tear part of my body off. . . ."[4]

After a torturer hurts one person, the next torture is easier to perform.

Modern Torture

Water is a popular tool for torturing. One method of torture that has been in the news is called "waterboarding." In this type of torture, a victim is strapped to a board. The torturer pours water over the victim's face.

Sometimes a cloth or hood is over the victim's head. The victim believes he is drowning.

A rapporteur is a person who investigates and reports on a specific issue. Often that issue involves human rights. The UN Special Rapporteur has classified rape and other forms of sexual violence against women as forms of torture. This classification meets the standards of the UNCAT. It causes severe pain and suffering on purpose. The Special Rapporteur added one more part to the torture

An Iraqi man holds up a drill and a saw, torture tools used during the Persian Gulf War.

definition: powerlessness. For example, a guard has total power over his prisoner. If a victim cannot escape, he or she is made to feel powerless.

Torture can also be mental and psychological. Humiliation, watching someone else being tortured, or being forced to torture or kill someone else leaves no physical marks on a person. But mentally, the scars are just as deep as those that physical torture leaves on the skin.

Chapter 3

THE EFFECTS OF TORTURE

*B*eing tortured to death must be one of the worst ways to die. But not everyone who is tortured dies. The victims of torture who do survive have deep scars to overcome. Some of these scars are visible, such as physical scars or other injuries. Physical symptoms might need treatment. These include broken bones, loss of hearing or sight, long-lasting headaches, or paralyzed muscles. Some of these injuries will heal with proper care. Others may never heal and will be a constant reminder to the victim.

Physical scarring is not the only effect of torture. Other scars are invisible. These scars are mental. Some survivors feel guilty about escaping the torture and leaving behind loved ones who might still be tortured. Other victims are depressed and may be suicidal. The Center for Victims of Torture (CVT) reports other effects on victims. Some torture survivors vomit when they eat. Others have panic attacks because of loud noises. Some of the CVT's clients have sleep-related problems. And some clients cannot sleep in the dark because it brings back the horrible memories of when they were tortured.

According to the same report, children of torture victims have problems related to their parents' treatment. Even years after their parents' torture, they have more emotional problems than other

The scars on this victim's hip were caused by pepper spray and tear gas.

children. They may have behavior problems, sudden mood changes, or learning problems. They might exhibit violent play or artwork. They might have a lot of fear and anxiety. Or they might complain about feeling sick or in pain. They might avoid anything that reminds them of an upsetting event in their lives or their parents' lives.

Effects on Torturers

The bad effects on torture victims are clear. What many people do not think about is the effect of torture on the torturers. One's sense of kindness and understanding are important in recognizing another person's pain.

Treating Solitary Children

Many children arrive at treatment centers having been separated from their parents. One treatment center in the United Kingdom "has seen an increasing number of unaccompanied children, many under the age of 12, being referred" for treatment.[1] These children might have been tortured or seen torture. They also must deal with being away from their parents. That situation adds another piece to the puzzle of treating children.

However, torturers must hold back their concern. In the process, they often become less sensitive to others' pain in general. It also becomes more difficult for torturers to know right from wrong. They lose their "moral compass." Plus, the more someone commits torture, the more likely that person is to commit torture in the future. Torturers also tend to lose respect for human dignity through their actions. Each instance of torture makes the next easier to commit.

Some suggest that only "bad" people would commit torture. Research such as the Stanford Prison Experiment suggests this is not the case. It shows that with the right conditions, normal, "good" people will become active torturers. In the 1971 experiment, 24 college students were paid to act as either "prisoners" or "guards." After only six days, the experiment was ended. The behavior and attitudes of the guards had changed very much. Both groups seemed to feel they were in an actual prison. The guards, having been given power, quickly turned to evil actions over their prisoners.

Leonor La Rosa was an army intelligence agent in Lima, Peru. She was tortured by fellow agents who thought she had leaked information to the media. She was left with severe spine damage. She now has difficulty performing simple tasks.

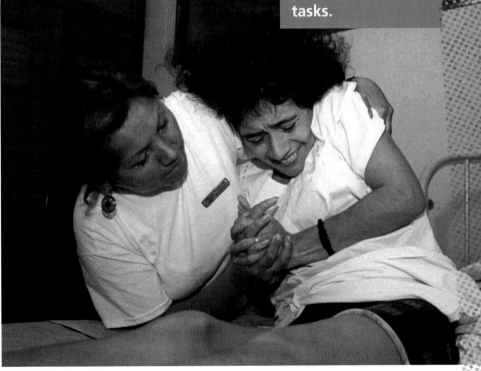

Philip Zimbardo created that experiment. He later wrote, "Human behavior is much more under the control of situational forces than most of us recognize or want to acknowledge . . . many of us can be morphed into creatures alien to our usual natures."[2]

In other words, in certain conditions, even "good" people might behave in terrible ways. This same effect can happen to torturers who otherwise are normal members of society.

After the Stanford experiment was over, Zimbardo wrote about the participants' discussions. He said the group tried to talk about the conflicts. They tried to think of other things that would help people act better in real-life situations. Zimbardo believed that the experiment helped the participants. They were able to think of ways people in their situation

"Doing Nothing"

Some of the "guards" for the Stanford Prison Experiment did not take part in mistreating their "prisoners." However, they also did not act to stop bad treatment. Edmund Burke, an English philosopher, once said, "The only thing necessary for the triumph of evil is for good men to do nothing."[3]

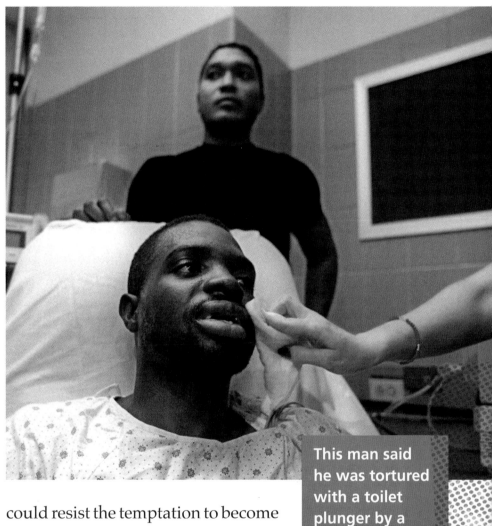

This man said he was tortured with a toilet plunger by a police officer in Brooklyn, New York.

could resist the temptation to become "evil."

Effects on Societies

When torture becomes accepted in society, the entire population suffers. The power of the state becomes less respected by its citizens. This

Effects of
torture on a
society, such as
this community
in Iraq, can be
negative and
strong.

is because the power is based on force rather than truth and justice. Then, torture is likely to cause conflict between those who believe it is wrong and those who think it is useful in some situations. Torture can be an easier way to gain information than thoughtful and time-consuming research. Investigations that rely on torture are less likely to be thorough. When torture becomes the norm, "the quality of investigations tends to be low. Careful marshalling of evidence is replaced by beating up suspects."[4] Information gained through torture is not always correct.

Treatment of Torture Victims

One of the United States' most-respected organizations to help treat the tortured is the Center for Victims of Torture (CVT). Founded in 1985, it has centers in Minneapolis and Saint Paul, Minnesota, Washington DC, Sierra Leone, Liberia, and the Democratic Republic of Congo in Africa. Since its founding, other treatment centers around the United States have helped torture victims.

The first job is to heal any physical injuries. According to the CVT, "As their bodies heal, clients begin to believe that their minds can heal."[5] Next, mental-health specialists help these victims learn to talk about what happened to them. This can give the victims hope for the future.

The CVT's recovery process helps those who have been tortured by "healing the whole survivor."[6] The CVT names three stages of healing. The first is safety and balance. This stage helps the victim feel

Minneapolis
Saint Paul

UNITED STATES

Washington

SIERRA LEONE
Freetown
Monrovia
LIBERIA

DEM. REP.
OF CONGO

Lubumbashi

The Center for Victims of Torture seeks to provide counsel, care, and therapy to victims of torture. CVT has locations in the United States and Africa.

safe, become healthy, and learn to trust others. The second stage is grief and mourning. This stage helps victims deal with the mental pain of their torture. The third and final stage is reconnection. The goal of this stage is for the victim to return to living a normal life. This means working and learning to love people.

The length of treatment varies for each person. One study of CVT patients in the early 1990s showed an average length of treatment to be about 18 months.

Felix, left, was captured in Uganda. Children like him are kidnapped and forced to become soldiers or sex slaves. He is beginning to recover.

Chapter 4

THE ETHICS OF TORTURE

Almost every country in the world publicly disapproves of torture. The United Nations and its member countries condemn those countries that do use it. Democracies such as the United Kingdom and the United States have condemned its use for hundreds of years.

But despite this, torture is still widespread. Amnesty International monitors human rights abuses worldwide. A report conducted between 1997 and 2000 showed that torture was reported in 150 of 195 countries surveyed. It showed that "[i]n more than 70 [countries], they [reported that tortures] were widespread or persistent. In more than 80 countries, people reportedly died as a result."[1]

Torture is not only used in dictatorships such as Saddam Hussein's Iraq. Torture has also been found in democracies such as Israel and India. At different

Torture in Iraq

Manfred Nowak is a Special Rapporteur for the United Nations. Nowak reported in September 2006 that the torture in Iraq might have been worse after Saddam Hussein's fall than before. Many refugees fleeing the country bear many physical marks of severe torture.

times, certain types of torture have been legal in both of these countries. According to Darius Rejali, a writer from Iran, "torture has always happened in democracies . . . even Britain, France and America were torturing in their colonies. . . ."[2]

However, many people who study ethics agree that torture is always wrong. They believe it is wrong for many different reasons.

Many people object to torture on the grounds that it is morally wrong. They view it as treating victims as things rather than as people. Torturers make their victims seem less than human on purpose. This condition makes it easier to mistreat and torture them.

Even people who do not reject torture for moral reasons may object on other grounds. Torture has long been thought of as useless in gaining good information. Victims of torture face great physical and mental pain. These things make it almost impossible to remain silent. However, the information they provide may be wrong. Or it may be only what the torturers want to hear in order to bring an end to the pain. The victims figure out what their torturers want and will say it, even if

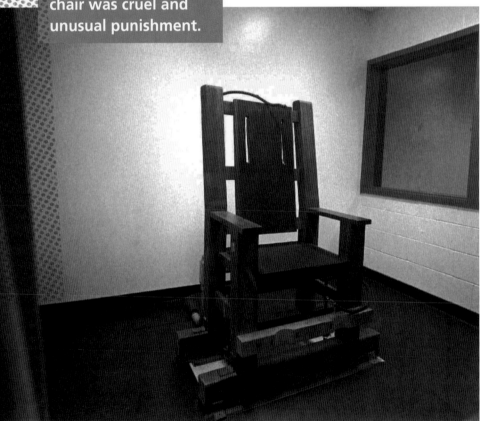

This image shows an electric chair used for the execution of prisoners in Nebraska. One prisoner brought charges against the prison by saying that use of the electric chair was cruel and unusual punishment.

they are lying. This means the torturer cannot be sure what the truth is. If the torturer thinks the person has more information, the torture may continue. But to get information, there are other good ways to question people that do not involve torture.

Professional Ethics

Many groups have objected to torture based on their professional beliefs. These groups have agreed never to take part in torture. The American Psychological Association (APA), for example, has condemned torture. The APA also reminds psychologists that "the psychologist shall attempt to intervene to stop such behavior."[3]

In 2006 the World Medical Association (WMA) made a promise similar to the APA's. The WMA's vow states doctors should not help with torture in any way. A doctor's main purpose is to help people with physical illness. Torture goes against a doctor's goals. It causes people physical pain. The WMA recognizes that physicians practice in dangerous areas of the world. A government might order a physician to take part in torture. The physician may refuse because it is the wrong thing to do. But by rejecting the torture or other cruel treatment, the doctor might be in danger. The doctor's life or the lives of his family members might be threatened.

The War on Terror

Current opinions about the ethics of torture commonly involve questioning suspected terrorists. The Bush administration argued that terrorists were not part of any country's army. Therefore, they did not have to be treated according to the laws against torture. The administration also says that rules against torture were written before terrorism became common. Some say that this means the rules do not apply to today's issues.

Opponents of torture point out that allowing it fuels the enemy. In this case, the enemy is the terrorist.

Public Opinion

An article in the *Washington Post* revealed the thoughts of the American public on the use of torture. According to their findings, most Americans are against torturing terrorists. But the public did not always agree if some means of physical pressure are allowable. The majority rejected all forms of sexual humiliation, use of electricity or water, and physical beatings. But many accepted the possible use of sleep deprivation or loud music.

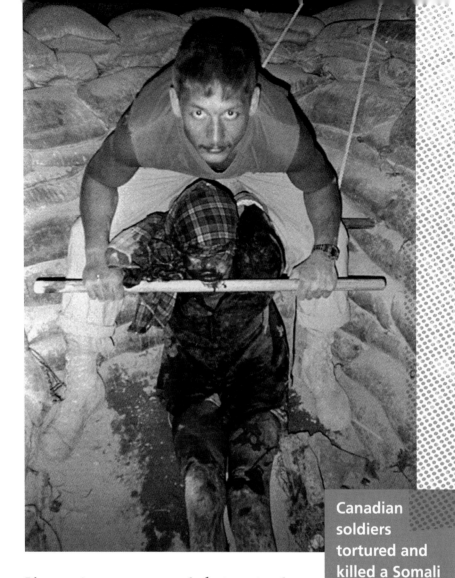

Canadian soldiers tortured and killed a Somali civilian at a peacekeeping camp in 1993.

If terrorists are tortured, their attitudes can harden further. They might want revenge against the torturing country. Finally, one goal of U.S. policies around the world is to win the "hearts and minds" of people. The United States wants others to trust that it is a beacon of individual freedoms. When the U.S. government allows torture, it loses this

It is believed that these are the bodies of men executed by Saddam Hussein's government. They were suspected of being spies.

battle for the hearts and minds of other countries. People may look at U.S. actions. They may decide the nation cannot be trusted and does not mean what it says.

Some people have argued in support of torture. They use the "ticking bomb" argument. This says that in some cases, it is worth harming one person to save the lives of many. For example, assume a terrorist group declared that it had put a bomb in a major city. The government captures a known leader of the group.

The leader can provide the location of the bomb but refuses to give that information. Torture is viewed as the only method of getting the information quickly enough to stop the bomb.

Those who support torture in this case say it is an okay trade-off. By torturing one man or his friends and family, information could be gotten that would save thousands of people.

Renditions

The U.S. government listens to world opinion. The government wants to earn and keep respect through its actions. This means that the desire for information—sometimes illegally gained—may conflict with statements against torture.

One way to solve this has been through the use of renditions. This means sending a terror suspect from one country to another for questioning. For example, a suspected terrorist being held in the United States may not be tortured because of laws against it. But the suspect may be sent to another country. Egypt, for example, does not have laws against torture. The Egyptians could torture the suspect and provide U.S. officials with any information they gathered during the torture process.

These secret, illegal camps used for renditions are called "black sites." By using them, a government

What Is Rendition?

"Rendition: **Kidnapping terrorist suspects and delivering them to a foreign country for trial. In 'extraordinary rendition,' suspects are 'lent' to a foreign country for interrogation and torture."[4]**

—Phil Edwards, "Torture: Definitions."

such as the United States can state that it has not tortured anyone. However, the government still receives the "benefits" of the torture—which is to gain information or a confession.

Chapter 5

PREVENTING TORTURE

The United States has laws against torture that date back to 1791. This is when the Bill of Rights was enacted. These ten amendments to the U.S. Constitution include the Eighth Amendment. It states: "cruel and unusual punishments [shall not be] inflicted" on any person who has been arrested.[1] The intent is clear: no prisoner shall be mistreated. This includes torture.

U.S. laws condemn torture. The United States has signed the Convention against Torture that states torture anywhere, for any reason, is illegal. It specifically mentions that a state of national emergency is not reason to torture a person for information. Human Rights Watch notes that "torture cannot be justified by exceptional circumstances, nor can it be excused on the basis of an order from a superior officer."[2] People who torture will be placed on trial as laws allow. For example, a U.S. law exists that can punish torturers with up to 20 years in jail. The one committing the torture may receive the death penalty if the torture victim dies.

The U.S. military has been under fire for its use of torture. The military's handbook also outlaws torture: "The use of force, mental torture, threats, insults, or exposure to unpleasant and inhumane treatment of any kind is prohibited by law and is neither authorized nor condoned by the US Government. . . . [T]he use of force is a poor technique, as it yields unreliable results, may damage subsequent collection efforts, and can induce the source to say whatever he thinks the interrogator wants to hear."[3]

In other words, the U.S. military should not torture its prisoners. Government personnel may, however, use other nonviolent methods and tricks during questioning.

International Laws

The English Bill of Rights and the French Declaration of the Rights of Man explain what rights all people have. Along with these documents, several other international documents are known for their stands against torture. The main documents include:

- The Universal Declaration of Human Rights (UDHR) (1948)

The United Nations has taken steps toward defining and ending torture.

- The Third and Fourth Geneva Conventions (ratified in 1949)
- The United Nations Convention against Torture and Other Cruel, Inhuman or Degrading Treatment or Punishment (UNCAT) (1984)
- Inter-American Convention to Prevent and Punish Torture (1987)

The 1945 UN charter says that all people are equal and should not be mistreated. But World War II showed the horrors of the Nazi government's actions against people. It made the world aware that a document was needed that stated exactly the rights of every human. The UN adopted the Universal Declaration of Human Rights in late 1948. This declaration is not a treaty. But it is important for the stand it takes against mistreatment of all human beings. Article 5 states, "No one shall be subjected to torture or to cruel, inhuman or degrading treatment or punishment."[4] The declaration has influenced the way many national constitutions are set up.

The Geneva Conventions are named for Geneva, Switzerland. That is where they were first enacted. The first convention was signed in 1864. The conventions were originally set up to protect prisoners who had been captured during wartime. They also were meant to protect the wounded and provide for humane treatment. They specified other behaviors during wartime. These included protecting hospitals, medical transport, civilians, and others who are not part of military forces. Most countries have signed the conventions. They bind themselves to follow

Geneva Convention

"The following acts are and shall remain prohibited . . . : violence to life and person, in particular murder of all kinds, mutilation, cruel treatment and torture."[5]
—*Article 3 of the Third Geneva Convention, 1949*

their articles. The U.S. military has followed their rules in the past. However, since the terror attacks of September 11, 2001, the military has argued that the conventions do not apply to certain terrorists.

The UN Convention against Torture (UNCAT) document took effect June 26, 1987. Its goals were to outlaw torture and other mistreatment. The Committee against Torture was created to watch whether countries are following the convention. Countries that signed the convention must regularly report to the committee regarding human rights conditions. The committee can also look into complaints. And it can visit prisons to see how prisoners are treated.

Purposes

"Torture shall be understood to be any act intentionally performed whereby physical or mental pain or suffering is inflicted on a person for purposes of criminal investigation, as a means of intimidation, as personal punishment, as a preventive measure, as a penalty, or for any other purpose."[6]

—*Inter-American Convention to Prevent and Punish Torture*

An antiwar protest in London

The Inter-American Convention to Prevent and Punish Torture uses a similar definition of torture as the UNCAT. However, it adds one additional condition: "Torture shall also be understood to be the use of methods upon a person intended to . . . diminish his physical or mental capacities, even if they do not cause physical pain or mental anguish."[7] Any techniques that intend to change the victim's personality or attitudes are also considered torture.

Truth Commissions

The government's official use of torture has come to an end in some countries that previously used torture. In South Africa, this happened by a peaceful change of government. In Iraq, it happened because Saddam Hussein was forcefully removed from power. In Iraq, people ask what should happen to those who tortured others. Should the torturers be punished? Should members of that government be imprisoned? These actions seem fair. Yet history shows that few torturers are successfully put on trial and convicted.

Some new governments have tried a different method. They set up truth commissions. Guatemala, Argentina, and Haiti have tried to use these commissions to help their countries begin to heal. These commissions are similar to trials. Tortured people can testify about what happened to them. Those who inflicted torture can confess what they did. The difference is that the torturers are promised that they will not be punished if they confess fully.

South Africa has had one of the most successful experiences with its Truth and Reconciliation Commission. These hearings "presented torturers and killers sitting on stage, under oath, answering days of questions from lawyers, commissioners, and even directly from their former victims."[8] But the former torturers and killers had motivation to confess. If they told the whole truth, they were offered official forgiveness. They also had to prove that their crimes were committed for political reasons.

Not all of these commissions have been equally successful. However, by focusing on torture in the past, these commissions hope their work will help heal their nations.

Take Action

Being aware of torture and doing something about it are different

According to the United States Institute of Peace, Truth Commissions have been set up in the highlighted countries.

things. It is nearly impossible to imagine being tortured. William Schulz believes that "for most Americans torture is so alien. Is it easier to imagine your home destroyed in a fire or a storm or an earthquake than to imagine yourself being held in a six- by eight-foot cell and tortured day and night? It is indeed and that is one reason disaster relief

Cyrus Cylinder: Oldest Declaration of Human Rights

The UN Convention against Torture (UNCAT) is an important document. So are the British Magna Carta of 1215 and the U.S. Constitution written in 1787. Long before any of these documents, however, came the "first charter of human rights."[10] The Cyrus Cylinder is a piece of clay from ancient Babylon. The king of Persia, Cyrus, wrote laws on the clay. It describes how he conquered Babylon and how its residents were to be treated. Cyrus allowed people whom the Babylonians had enslaved to return to their homelands. He also restored temples and religious shrines in neighboring countries.

receives so many more dollars than human rights."[9]

Perhaps it is time to change that attitude. It is easy to ignore or disregard torture. Few of us have contact with tortured people.

Protestors gather in Portland, Oregon, in an event sponsored by Amnesty International.

You can take action to help prevent torture. Write to members of Congress. Ask them not to support the use of torture. Volunteer with a justice group such as Amnesty International. Contribute to a recovery center such as the Center for Victims of Torture. To help change the attitudes regarding torture, this may be the most important time to become involved.

Glossary

Bill of Rights
The first ten amendments to the U.S. Constitution; it includes the right that prisoners shall not be subjected to "cruel and unusual" punishments.

Black Sites
Illegal camps for holding terrorists for questioning.

Convention
A set of rules.

Human Rights
Rights that are considered to belong to everyone at all times and in all places.

Inquisition
A period during the Middle Ages when the Roman Catholic Church and governments investigated "wrong" religious beliefs.

Interrogation
A session of intense questioning.

Rendition

The act of sending suspected terrorists to a third country for questioning; using renditions is sometimes an attempt to avoid laws against torture.

Spanish Inquisition

An inquisition in Spain originally conducted to discover secret Jews; this was not part of the European Inquisition.

"Ticking Bomb" Argument

An imaginary scenario that questions if it is worth torturing one person to get information that might save thousands of lives.

Torture

Applying physical and mental pain to gain information from, or control over, someone who is unable to resist.

Waterboarding

Placing a victim on a board and continually pouring water over the victim's face to simulate drowning.

More Information

Books

Banks, Deena. *Amnesty International*. Milwaukee, WI: World Almanac Library, 2004.

Berry, Joy. *Mine and Yours: Human Rights for Kids*. New York: PowerHouse Books, 2005.

Burger, Leslie, and Debra L. Rahm. *United Nations High Commissioner for Refugees: Making a Difference in Our World*. Minneapolis, MN: Lerner, 1996.

Kramer, Ann. *Human Rights: Who Decides?* Chicago: Heinemann, 2007.

Web Sites

Amnesty International USA (www.amnestyusa.org). Amnesty International is an organization of people who are devoted to the fight for human rights.

BBC Online—"Ethical Issues: Torture." (www.bbc.co.uk/religion/ethics/torture/). This BBC news site discusses the ethics of torture. The site also documents recent news and legislation regarding torture.

Center for Victims of Torture (www.cvt.org). The Center for Victims of Torture offers healing services to torture survivors.

Notes

Chapter 1. What Is Torture?

1. "Torture." *World Book Online*. 25 May 2008 <http://www.worldbookonline.com/wb/Article?id=ar562140&st=torture>.
2. "Convention against Torture and Other Cruel, Inhuman or Degrading Treatment or Punishment." U.N. Office of the High Commissioner for Human Rights. Part I, Article 1. 25 May 2008 <http://www.unhchr.ch/html/menu3/b/h_cat39.htm>.
3. "Torture." *Stanford Encyclopedia of Philosophy*. 5 Jan. 2008. 18 July 2008 <http://plato.stanford.edu/entries/torture/>.
4. U.S. Department of State Bulletin. *U.S. signs UN convention against torture*. 20 May 1988. <http://findarticles.com/p/articles/mi_m1079/is_n2137_v88/ai_6742034>.
5. "Torture." *Stanford Encyclopedia of Philosophy*. 5 Jan. 2008. 18 July 2008 <http://plato.stanford.edu/entries/torture/>.
6. "About Torture." *Amnesty International USA*. 25 May 2008 <http://www.amnestyusa.org/Reports-Statements-and-Issue-Briefs/About-Torture/page.do?id=1031032&n1=3&n2=38&n3=1052>.
7. "Survivors of Politically Motivated Torture: A Large, Growing, and Invisible Population of Crime Victims." *U.S. Department of Justice, Office for Victims of Crime*. 30 July 2008 <http://www.ojp.usdoj.gov/ovc/publications/infores/motivatedtorture/welcome.html>.
8. Ibid.

Chapter 2. A History of Torture

1. Fordham University. "Medieval Sourcebook: Witchcraft Documents."15 July 2008 <http://www.fordham.edu/halsall/source/witches1.html>.
2. "Inquisition." *World Book Online*. 15 July 2008 <http://www.worldbookonline.com/wb/Article?id=ar277240&st=inquisition>.

3. "Torquemada, Tomas de." *World Book Online*. 20 Apr. 2008. <http://www.worldbookonline.com/wb/Article?id=ar561780&st=t orquemada>.

4. William F. Schulz, ed. *The Phenomenon of Torture: Readings and Commentary*. Philadelphia: University of Pennsylvania Press, 2007. 336.

Chapter 3. The Effects of Torture

1. Medical Foundation for the Care of Victims. "Children and Adolescents." 19 Apr. 2008 <http://www.torturecare.org.uk/about_us/24>.

2. Philip G. Zimbardo. "Power turns good soldiers into 'bad apples.'" *Boston Globe*. 9 May 2004. <http://www.boston.com/news/globe/editorial_opinion/oped/articles/2004/05/09/power_turns_good_soldiers_into_bad_apples/>.

3. The Columbia World of Quotations. 18 Apr. 2008 <http://www.bartleby.com/66/18/9118.html>.

4. "Torture." *Stanford Encyclopedia of Philosophy*. 5 Jan. 2008. 18 July 2008 <http://plato.stanford.edu/entries/torture/>.

5. "Healing Services." *Center for Torture Victims*. 25 May 2008 <http://www.cvt.org/main.php/HealingServices/Minneapolis-St. Paul>.

6. "Survivors of Politically Motivated Torture: A Large, Growing, and Invisible Population of Crime Victims." *U.S. Department of Justice, Office for Victims of Crime*. 19 Mar. 2007. <http://www.ojp.usdoj.gov/ovc/publications/infores/motivatedtorture/welcome.html>.

Chapter 4. The Ethics of Torture

1. Amnesty USA. "About Torture." 15 July 2008 <http://www.amnestyusa.org/Reports-Statements-and-Issue-Briefs/About-Torture/page.do?id=1031032&n1=3&n2=38&n3=1052>.

2. "Torture and Democracy: Scholar Darius Rejali Details the Scope and History of Modern Torture." *Democracy Now! Online*. 12 Mar. 2008 <http://www.democracynow.org/2008/3/12/torture_and_democracy_scholar_darius_rejali>.

3. "Resolution Against Torture and Other Cruel, Inhuman, and Degrading Treatment or Punishment." *American Psychological Association.* 9 Aug. 2006. 25 May 2008 <http://www.apa.org/governance/resolutions/notortureres.html>.
4. Phil Edwards. "Torture: Definitions." 25 May 2008 <http://www.channel4.com/news/microsites/T/torture/defs.html>.

Chapter 5. Preventing Torture

1. "The Charters of Freedom: The Bill of Rights." *National Archives and Records Administration (NARA).* 15 July 2008 <http://www.archives.gov/exhibits/charters/bill_of_rights_transcript.html>.
2. "Summary of International and U.S. Law Prohibiting Torture and Other Ill-treatment of Persons in Custody." *Human Rights Watch.* 24 May 2004. 15 July 2008 <http://www.hrw.org/english/docs/2004/05/24/usint8614.htm>.
3. "Interrogation and the Interrogator." *U.S. Army Field Manual* 34-52. 15 July 2008 <http://www.globalsecurity.org/intell/library/policy/army/fm/fm34-52/>.
4. "All Human Rights for All: Fiftieth Anniversary of the Universal Declaration of Human Rights, 1948–1998." *United Nations.* 25 May 2008 <http://www.un.org/Overview/rights.html>.
5. International Committee of the Red Cross. "Convention (III) relative to the Treatment of Prisoners of War. Geneva, 12 August 1949." 19 Apr. 2008 <http://www.icrc.org/ihl.nsf/7c4d08d9b287a42141256739003e636b/6fef854a3517b75ac125641e004a9e68>.
6. "Inter-American Convention to Prevent and Punish Torture." *Organization of American States, Department of International Law. Article 2.* 15 July 2008 <http://www.oas.org/juridico/English/Treaties/a-51.html>.
7. Ibid.
8. Schulz, William F., ed. *The Phenomenon of Torture: Readings and Commentary.* Philadelphia: University of Pennsylvania Press, 2007. 338.
9. Ibid.
10. British Museum. "Forgotten Empire: The World of Ancient Persia." 19 Apr. 2008 <http://www.thebritishmuseum.ac.uk/forgottenempire/legacy/cylinder.html>.

Index

About the Author

Charles Pederson is a consulting editor, writer, and translator. He has written for and contributed to many fiction and nonfiction publications for both children and adults. A graduate in linguistics, international relations, and German, he has traveled widely, bringing to his work an appreciation of different peoples and cultures. He and his family live near Minneapolis, Minnesota.

Photo Credits